EARTH ROCKS!
LANDSLIDES

BY SARA GILBERT

CREATIVE EDUCATION • CREATIVE PAPERBACKS

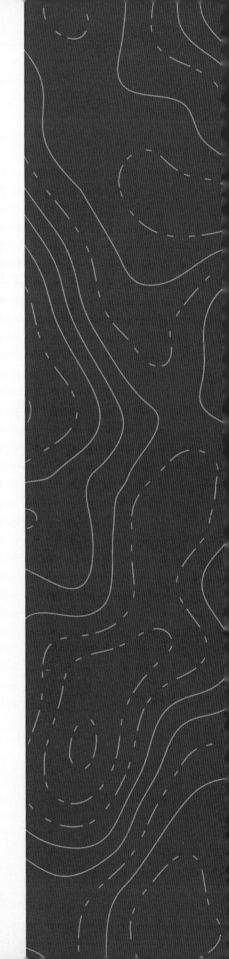

Published by Creative Education and Creative Paperbacks
P.O. Box 227, Mankato, Minnesota 56002
Creative Education and Creative Paperbacks are
imprints of The Creative Company
www.thecreativecompany.us

Design by Chelsey Luther; **production by** Joe Kahnke
Art direction by Rita Marshall
Printed in the United States of America

Photographs by Alamy (imageBROKER, David Keith Jones, Pulsar
Images), Dreamstime (TMarchev), Science Source (Science Source),
Shutterstock (A_Lesik, jayk67, muratart, siete_vidas, TonyV3112, ian
woolcock), Spoon Graphics (Chris Spooner)

Library of Congress Cataloging-in-Publication Data
Names: Gilbert, Sara.
Title: Landslides / Sara Gilbert.
Series: Earth Rocks!
Includes bibliographical references and index.
Summary: An elementary exploration of landslides, focusing on the
geological evidence that helps explain how and where they form and
spotlighting famous examples, such as the 2013 Indian landslides.
Identifiers: ISBN 978-1-60818-895-6 (hardcover) / ISBN 978-1-62832-
511-9 (pbk) / ISBN 978-1-56660-947-0 (eBook)

This title has been submitted for CIP processing under LCCN
2017937621.

CCSS: RI.1.1, 2, 4, 5, 6, 7; RI.2.2, 5, 6, 7, 10; RI.3.1, 5, 7, 8; RF.1.1, 3, 4; RF.2.3, 4

First Edition HC 9 8 7 6 5 4 3 2 1
First Edition PBK 9 8 7 6 5 4 3 2 1

*Pictured on cover: Red sandstone cliffs, England (top); landslide near
Black Sea (bottom)*

TABLE OF CONTENTS

ROLLING ROCKS

You are standing at the bottom of a big hill. You hear a loud rumble. Rocks and dirt are falling down the hill. A landslide is coming. You need to get out of the way!

ON THE MOVE

A landslide is the movement of a large amount of dirt, rocks, and **debris** down a **slope**. Some landslides move slowly. They last many years.

Others happen quickly. A land-slide can move as fast as 200 miles (322 km) per hour!

STARTING THE SLIDE

Gravity makes landslides happen. But there are many events that can come right before a landslide.

Heavy rain or melting snow can cause a landslide. **Earthquakes** and **erupting** volcanoes can start them, too.

DESTRUCTIVE DEBRIS

There are many kinds of land-slides. Some of the most **destructive** are called debris flows. These can knock down trees and pick up cars. They can move entire houses.

STOPPING THE SLIDE

Landslides can happen any-where there are hills and mountains. Scientists work hard to tell when landslides will happen. They try to help people stop them.

WIRE NETTING

BRAZIL, 2011

DANGEROUS LANDSLIDES

In 2013, flooding in India caused several landslides. More than 5,000 people were killed. Near Rio de Janeiro, Brazil, landslides killed 900 people in 2011. A 2014 landslide in Oso, Washington, buried a neighborhood in mud.

Landslides leave their mark on hills and mountains. Are there hills where you live? See if they have ever had a landslide!

ACTIVITY: MAKE A LITTLE LANDSLIDE

Materials

Disposable aluminum baking pan

Potting soil or sand

Water

Toy trees, houses, and cars

Books

1. Fill the aluminum pan halfway with potting soil or sand. Build up more soil or sand at one end of the pan.

2. Place your toy trees, houses, and cars in the soil.

3. Slide your books under the built-up end of the pan to create more of a slope.

4. Start pouring water in the pan at the side that is propped up. Continue until the soil or sand starts sliding toward the other end of the pan. What happens to your toys as the soil moves?

GLOSSARY

debris: loose natural materials, including rocks, dirt, and leaves

destructive: causing lots of damage

earthquakes: sudden, violent shakings of the earth caused by the sliding of tectonic plates

erupting: for volcanoes, becoming active and ejecting lava, smoke, gas, and ash

gravity: the force that attracts objects toward the center of the earth

slope: a surface that is higher at one end than the other

READ MORE

Maurer, Daniel D. *Do You Really Want to Create a Mudslide?*
North Mankato, Minn.: Amicus, 2017.

Meister, Cari. *Landslides*. Minneapolis: Jump!, 2016.

WEBSITES

FEMA's Youth Preparedness Program: Landslides
https://www.ready.gov/kids/know-the-facts/landslides
Learn more about landslides and how to prepare for them.

Weather Wiz Kids: Landslides
http://www.weatherwizkids.com/?page_id=1326
Find answers to landslide questions and learn about the
different types of landslides.

Note: Every effort has been made to ensure that any websites listed above were active at
the time of publication and suitable for children. However, because of the nature of the
Internet, it is impossible to guarantee that these sites will remain active indefinitely or that
their contents will not be altered.

INDEX